Skool & Cross

A tropical musical

Book and lyrics by Jenifer Toksvig
Music by David Perkins

Samuel French — London
New York - Toronto - Hollywood

© 2004 BY JENIFER TOKSVIG (book and lyrics)

This play is fully protected under the Copyright Laws of the British Commonwealth of Nations, the United States of America and all countries of the Berne and Universal Copyright Conventions.

All rights including Stage, Motion Picture, Radio, Television, Public Reading, and Translation into Foreign Languages, are strictly reserved.

No part of this publication may lawfully be reproduced in ANY form or by any means — photocopying, typescript, recording (including video-recording), manuscript, electronic, mechanical, or otherwise—or be transmitted or stored in a retrieval system, without prior permission.

SAMUEL FRENCH LTD, 52 FITZROY STREET, LONDON W1T 5JR, or their authorized agents, issue licences to amateurs to give performances of this play on payment of a fee. **This fee is subject to contract and subject to variation at the sole discretion of Samuel French Ltd.**

Licences for amateur performances are issued subject to the understanding that it shall be made clear in all advertising matter that the audience will witness an amateur performance; that the names of the authors of the plays shall be included on all programmes; and that the integrity of the authors' work will be preserved.

The publication of this play does not imply that it is necessarily available for performance by amateurs or professionals, either in the British Isles or Overseas. Amateurs and professionals considering a production are strongly advised in their own interests to apply to the appropriate agents for consent before starting rehearsals or booking a theatre or hall.

ISBN 0 573 08124 7

SKOOL & CROSSBONES

First performed at the Yvonne Arnaud Theatre, Guildford on 11th June 1998 by the Yvonne Arnaud Youth Theatre ACT 2, with the following cast:

Islanders

Alexander	Jonathan Slater
Laura	Lucy Barwell
Cuffee	Ben Browning
Quashie	Max Southworth
Fafa	Matthew Veira
Ol' Manbo/Headmistress	Caroline Dooley
Balmy	Amanda Duffield
Beachy	Alice Cook
Cabbie	Sam Applin
Half Pint	Vicky Lazzari
Limba	Jo Wright
Mo-Mo	Marie Kenyan
Shake-Shake	Sarah Slater
Sharky	Robert Slater
Toaster	Natalie Bolding
Tootie-Frootie	Chloe Jones
Sun God	Jonathan Veira

Pirates

Captain George	Andrew Charles
First Mate	Philip Bishop
Scaredy-Cat	Kit Stokes
Angel Cake	Katy Thorncroft
Clever Clogs	Olivia Oldroyd
Cross Bones	Hannah Turner
Flap Jack	Tara Stokes
Fearless Fred	Madelaine Fenner
Forty Winks	James Martin
Numbskull	Laura Seymour
Oops	Lucy Willis
Rib Tickler	Jenny May
Tuck Shop	Jo Brady
Jolly Roger	Seamus Benson

(The Yvonne Arnaud Youth Theatre ACT 2 comprises local children aged between 7 and 14)

Directed by Julia Burgess
Assistant Director Jenifer Toksvig
Musical Director David Perkins
Lighting Design by John Harris
Sound Design by Dan Last
Set built by Seamus Benson

IMPORTANT INFORMATION

ALTERATIONS TO THE SCRIPT AND SCORE

If changes, additions or cuts to the show are required to make it work for a particular group, any proposed alterations MUST be approved by the authors before rehearsals commence. Approval can be sought via Samuel French Ltd or directly from the authors via email. An email link for Jenifer Toksvig and David Perkins can be found at their website: www.toksvigperkins.com

The authors are happy to provide suggestions for such things as song cuts, scene change music, additional character names, and so on. Making contact with them is easy, and they will consider any request. Making small changes this way is free of charge, and it turns an illegal alteration into a legal one.

COVER ILLUSTRATION

Please note that the cover illustration remains the copyright of the artist, Simon Pearsall. Permission MUST be obtained prior to use of this illustration for publicity purposes, programmes, website graphics, or for any other purpose. Please contact Samuel French Ltd for details.

DIRECTOR'S CREDIT

The original director, Julia Burgess, is the creator of the original staging referred to in this libretto, both in the stage directions and the Director's Notes. It is a condition of the performing licence that the following credit be used on all programmes and posters for *Skool & Crossbones*:

Originally directed and choreographed by Julia Burgess

VIDEO AND AUDIO RECORDING

In certain circumstances, permission may be given for a video or audio recording of your show to be made. Please apply to Samuel French Ltd for full details. Video and audio recordings made without prior permission are STRICTLY not allowed, even for archival or training purposes.

TOKSVIG-PERKINS MUSICALS

The authors' website at www.toksvigperkins.com has photographs of the original production, sound bites, and other useful information (including details of other shows written by Toksvig-Perkins). Jenifer and David welcome your comments about their shows, as well as photographs of your production, via email.

DIRECTOR'S NOTES

CHARACTER BREAKDOWN

The show can be easily adapted to suit the number of children you wish to have in the cast. There is no limit to the number in the Island or Pirate chorus

Sun God
The god of the sun can be played as a voice-over, either live on a microphone offstage, or pre-recorded and played back as a sound cue. (It is also possible to have an actor play this part onstage if required, although not as effective as a voice-over.)

Fafa
He is the Sun God's teenaged son. He struggles with his exams, his father and his responsibilities, but desperately longs to fulfil his destiny. He's enthusiastic, but isn't very steady on his Immortal feet yet. He has something to prove to his father, and now is his chance to prove it.
SONGS: The Spies (quintet); Tonight We Fight! (solo section); Calypso Carnival

Laura
She is a teenager and the granddaughter of the island's spiritual leader. She is a bit of a tomboy with a strong personality and is not afraid to try anything. She is someone that the others look up to.
SONGS: Tropical Island Rhythm; Prayer to the Gods (solo section); The Summoning of Fafa (solo section); The Spies (quintet); Tonight We Fight!; Calypso Carnival

Alexander
Similar to Laura, he is a teenager with a strong personality and the others admire him for that.
SONGS: Tropical Island Rhythm; Prayer to the Gods (solo section); The Summoning of Fafa; The Spies (quintet); Tonight We Fight!; Calypso Carnival

Cuffee and Quashie
They are slightly younger than the rest of the Islanders and they take the role of comedy duo. They are tearaway kids, who can be played by either boys or girls.
SONGS: Tropical Island Rhythm; Prayer to the Gods; The Summoning of Fafa; The Spies (quintet); Mumbo Jumbo (solo section); Tonight We Fight!; Calypso Carnival

Ol' Manbo/Headmistress
Technically, she's an adult, but she can and should be played by a young person if possible. She becomes the archetypal evil headmistress towards the end of the musical and this role should be played up as much as possible.
SONG: Calypso Carnival

Island Chorus
The chorus can range in age from six or seven up to teenage. They are generally down-to-earth young people who enjoy life on their island. A character name should be given to each Islander. Those from the original cast list can be used, or others created to suit the particular performers or production. Allowing cast members to choose their own character name may help them develop their character, which is just as important for the chorus as it is for the principal roles in this show.
SONGS: Tropical Island Rhythm; Prayer to the Gods; The Summoning of Fafa; Tonight We Fight!; Calypso Carnival

Captain George
He's trying to be the stereotypical Pirate, but is actually just a teenager with a vivid imagination and tons of energy. He's bossy and arrogant on the outside, but when confronted with authority, he crumbles.
SONGS: The Mutiny (solo section); A Pirate History; Mumbo Jumbo; Tonight We Fight! (solo section); Calypso Carnival

First Mate
He is a slightly younger kid, who will do anything the Captain says — this is hero-worshiping of the old-fashioned school-days variety. When Captain George crumbles, either the First Mate loses all his confidence, or that is the moment when he finds his own strength.
SONGS: The Mutiny; A Pirate History; Mumbo Jumbo (solo section); Tonight We Fight!; Calypso Carnival

Scaredy-Cat
He or she is a nervous kid, probably spoilt at home, and almost certainly one who was reluctant to try the whole Pirate thing. He or she followed along because there was no choice, and has regretted that ever since.
SONGS: The Mutiny; A Pirate History; Mumbo Jumbo (solo section); Tonight We Fight! (solo section); Calypso Carnival

Pirate Chorus
They should have distinct characteristics that show through in their Pirate name, e.g.: a clumsy pirate, a lazy pirate, and so on. A character name should be given to each Pirate. Those from the original cast list can be used, or others created to suit the particular performers or production. Allowing cast members to choose their own character name may help them develop their character, which is just as important for the chorus as it is for the principal roles in this show.
SONGS: The Mutiny; A Pirate History; Mumbo Jumbo; Tonight We Fight!; Calypso Carnival

SONG NOTES
(see also: Composer's Notes)

1. Tropical Island Rhythm
The opening number should have the feeling of the island awakening as the sun rises. The full company can play Islanders during this song, as **No. 1a Playout** is provided for half of the company to leave the stage and change into Pirate costumes. The tempo of this song should be bright and cheerful throughout.

2. Prayer to the Gods
This should start laid-back with a joyful reggae style and end with a contrasting sudden entrance of the Pirates. The staging style can be relaxed, with natural movement as opposed to strict choreography.

3. The Mutiny
A story is told throughout this song and, therefore, diction is very important. The Pirates should play the various characters referred to in the lyric, and the style of acting should be exaggerated and comical.

4. The Summoning of Fafa
This is a percussive and rhythmic number and should be both strong and precise in tempo. Choreography should be simple, to avoid confusion with the clapped accompaniment.

5. A Pirate History
A story is told in this number and the cast should be careful to avoid shouting or over-projecting the vocal line. The tempo of the song is bright and diction is important. As with *The Mutiny*, the acting style should be exaggerated and comical as the Pirates play characters from history. There are sections of this song that give smaller groups of Pirates the opportunity to show off their acting and singing skills.

6. The Spies
This song should have an air of intrigue and anticipation, in both performance and staging. Since there are fewer cast members involved in the number, staging should make full use of available stage space.

7. Mumbo Jumbo
This is a darker moment in the show and should have a sense of mystery and foreboding, both in staging and in performance.
8. Tonight We Fight!
Staging for this number should be fairly static since the lyric is complex and four-part harmony is required. There should be a choral feel to the vocal line.
9. Calypso Carnival
This song should have a Carnival party feeling throughout, and offers an opportunity for audience participation in a conga line!

SET

One simple set is all that's required, but the "Mumbo Jumbo" scene can be staged on the deck of the Pirate ship if another setting is desired.

A separate area of the stage that is not part of the island is required for Fafa when he speaks to his father, the Sun God. This can be achieved with lighting

The following items of scenery are suggested:
A pirate galleon (on a truck)
A small hut (only entrance/exit required, no interior)
Market stalls with appropriate set dressing
Palm trees and tropical flowers
Crates and barrels
A smiling sun (flown upstage)
Stage floor painted to indicate a beach shoreline

FURNITURE AND PROPERTIES

A list of properties can be found on Page 43. Many are essential to the show. However, they can be as simple or as elaborate as resources allow.

COSTUME

A suggested costume plot is indicated on Page 44. Costumes can be simplified according to the available resources.

LIGHTING AND EFFECTS

Thunder and lightning effects are essential to the show, and must be used as noted in the stage directions throughout the script.

With thanks to Julia Burgess for her original staging and direction.

COMPOSER'S NOTES

The metronome markings should be followed as closely as possible. The tempo for each number goes a long way towards determining the style and feeling of the song. A 'Calypso Carnival' that was too slow would sap the energy at the end of the show, when spirits should be at their highest and a "Spies" song that was too fast would lose its sense of intrigue, and so on.

Skool & Crossbones has been scored for piano, bass guitar, drums, trumpet in Bb, and alto sax — trebling flute and clarinet in Bb. A keyboard could be used to add extra sounds, for example steel drums in Nos. 1, 2 & 9, extra brass in Nos. 5, 6, 8 & 9, and even special effects in Nos. 7 & 8b, or to enhance thunder and lightning effects throughout the show. An electric or acoustic guitar could also be added, playing from the chord symbols in the piano/vocal score. Extra percussion, such as Guiros, Cabasas and Rain Sticks, could be played by members of the company, especially in Nos. 1, 4, 7 & 9. The piano/vocal score and the band parts are available on hire from Samuel French Ltd.

If necessary, the show could be performed with a reduced line-up, the minimum being piano and drums, with added percussion from the company.

David Perkins

MUSICAL NUMBERS

No. 1 Tropical Island Rhythm — Islanders
No. 1a Playout
No. 2 Prayer to the Gods — Alexander, Laura, Islanders
No. 3 The Mutiny — Captain George, Pirates
No. 4 The Summoning of Fafa — Laura, Islanders
No. 5 A Pirate History — All Pirates
No. 5a Exit of Pirates
No. 6 The Spies — Fafa, Alexander, Laura, Cuffee, Quashie
No. 6a Scene Change Music
No. 7 Mumbo Jumbo Cuffee, Quashie, First Mate, Scaredy-Cat, Pirates
No. 8 Tonight We Fight! — Full company
No. 8a Dialogue Underscore
No. 8b Ol' Manbo's Transformation I
No. 8c Ol' Manbo's Transformation II
No. 9 Calypso Carnival — Ol' Manbo, Full Company
No. 9a Curtain Calls
No 9b Encore (Reprise: Calypso Carnival) — Full Company
No 9c Exit Music

Piano/score and band parts available on hire from Samuel French Ltd

ACKNOWLEDGEMENTS

Jenifer "Words" Toksvig and David "Music" Perkins
would like to thank the following people for their continuous support :

Our "Whatever you write, we love it" families and friends.
The Yvonne Arnaud "Home Sweet Home" Theatre, Guildford.
James "I trust you with my theatre" Barber.
Seamus "I want to build a Pirate Galleon so write a show about pirates" Benson.
The ACT 2 "Of course we can do four-part harmony" kids (and their parents!)
Ellie "I wrote a bit of this show" Jones.
Caroline "Of the trees" Dooley.
"Thank the gods for" John Harris.
The very creative Simon "Comedy & Cartoons" Pearsall.

... and last but most importantly...

Julia "Simply lovely in every way" Burgess

Other musicals with book and lyrics by Jenifer Toksvig
and music by David Perkins,
published by Samuel French Ltd:

The Curious Quest for the Sandman's Sand
Shake, Ripple & Roll
Pandemonium! (a Greek Myth-adventure)

Also by David Perkins (with Caroline Dooley)
published by Samuel French Ltd:

The Selfish Giant
A chlidren's musical
based on the short story by Oscar Wilde

For our parents:
Julie & Claus
Anita & Ben

SKOOL & CROSSBONES

A Caribbean island. It is dawn

The stage represents the shoreline of the island; both beach and sea are visible. On the beach there are a few palm trees, tropical flowers, some market stalls and crates and barrels scattered around. A flag with a bright yellow sun on a bright orange background hangs from one of the market stalls. To one side of the stage is a small hut. Outside the hut is a stool with a large book next it and a wooden broom

When the play begins a breeze blows softly through the trees. The waves lap gently at the beach

Ol' Manbo is sweeping outside the door of her hut. She wears a long, full skirt and apron

Gradually, the Islanders, with Laura, Alexander, Cuffee and Quashie, begin to wander on to the stage and set up for the day. They place crates of fruit and vegetables, fish, hats and strings of bright flowers on to the market stalls. Some of them chat or play games. Some play percussion instruments, mimicking the sounds of nature and the rhythms of the island. They continue with all of these activities throughout the song

No. 1 Tropical Island Rhythm

All (*singing*)   Hear the dawn,
Full of laughter.
Feel the breeze,
Chasing after.
Hummingbird,
Sing a song now
And the gods will
Sing along now.

Silver moon,
See her falling.
Golden sun,
Hear him calling
Over the sea,
Summoning me.

Tropical island rhythm,
Carry me from the night time.
Tropical island rhythm,
Dance me through the day.

Rolling sea,
Gently flowing.
Summer breeze,
Feel it blowing.

Mockingbird,
Better fly now
And the gods will
Lift you high now.

Coconut,
In the palm tree,
Calabash,
High above me.
Fall to the sand. (*This is an instruction to the coconut and the calabash*)
Call to the land.

Tropical island rhythm,
Carry me from the night time.
Tropical island rhythm,
Dance me through the day.

God of the sunlight, come and shine upon me.
Sweet mama earth, won't you protect my family?
From the evening to the morning light,
Through the winter to the summer bright.
God of the harvest, won't you bring me plenty?
Old papa fire, now don't you leave me lonely.
Tropical island rhythm, dance me through the day.

The Islanders divide into two singing groups

Group 1	Hear the dawn,	**Group 2**	God of sunlight,
	Full of laughter.		Come and shine upon me.
	Feel the breeze,		Sweet mama earth,
	Chasing after.		Won't you protect my family?
	Hummingbird,		From the evening,
	Sing a song now		To the morning light,
	And the gods will		Through the winter
	Sing along now		To the summer bright.

Skool & Crossbones

Group 1	Silver moon, See her falling. Golden sun, Hear him calling Over the sea, Summoning me.	**Group 2**	God of the harvest, Won't you bring me plenty? Old papa fire, Now don't you leave me lonely. Keep the rhythm free, Summoning me.

All   Tropical island rhythm,
Carry me from the night time.
Tropical island rhythm,
Dance me through the day.

Tropical island rhythm,
Carry me from the night time.
Tropical island rhythm,
Dance me through the day.

Dance me through the day.

Music underscoring (No 1a. Playout)

The Islanders begin to set up, laying out gifts of fruit and other items for a ritual prayer to the Sun God. Ol' Manbo sits on a stool quietly in one corner, reading the large book

Fafa, a small boy, enters and moves to stand alone at the side of the stage

Fafa is separated from the main action, either with scenery or lighting. If lighting separates him, then the main state dips and a special comes up. He speaks to the Sun God, his father. The Sun God is only heard and is never seen. [See Director's Notes on page v]

Fafa Happy day of the sun, dad.
Sun God (*voice over*) Why, thank you, Fafa.
Fafa They're setting up a ceremony for you down on the island.
Sun God (*voice over*) I hope they remember to offer gifts to all the gods. Last week they forgot a few. It took me three days to calm down the god of bananas.
Fafa But it's the day of the sun. That's just you, right?
Sun God (*voice over*) Technically, yes, but it's all about team-work. You wanted to ask me a question, didn't you?
Fafa Me? No, I was just saying that they're setting up a ceremony …
Sun God (*voice over*) Fafa?

Fafa Yes?
Sun God (*voice over*) I'm omniscient. It means I know everything.
Fafa I know. I hate that.

The focus returns to the Island or the lighting changes

Ol' Manbo puts down her book on a stool and goes into her hut

Laura Alexander, whose turn is it to set up for the ceremony this week?
Alexander Cuffee and Quashie's.
Cuffee No, it's not!
Quashie It's not, Laura! We did it last week!
An Islander We did it last week!
Another Islander Yeah, it's definitely your turn!
Cuffee How about Ol' Manbo?
Quashie Yeah, why doesn't Ol' Manbo ever help?
Alexander Because Ol' Manbo spends all day reading big old books and being mean to us, that's why.
Laura Get on with it, you two.
Cuffee What's in those books, anyway?

During the following, Cuffee and Quashie push each other alternately up to Ol' Manbo's hut

Quashie If you're so curious, Cuffee, why don't you go and look? (*He pushes Cuffee*)
Cuffee You look, Quashie. (*He pushes Quashie*)
Quashie You. (*He pushes Cuffee*)
Cuffee No, you. (*He pushes Quashie*)
Quashie You! (*He pushes Cuffee*)

Ol' Manbo comes storming out of her hut

Ol' Manbo Get out of here! You stay away from my house!

Cuffee and Quashie run. Ol' Manbo sits back down with her book

The focus returns to Fafa or the lighting changes

Sun God (*voice over*) Come on then. Hit me with it.
Fafa "Hit me with it?" You've been watching too much TV.
Sun God (*voice over*) I'm just keeping up with the times. So hit me with it.

Fafa With what?
Sun God (*voice over*) Your big question!
Fafa Look, Cuffee and Quashie are arguing again ...

The focus switches back to the Island or the lighting changes

Cuffee and Quashie are fighting about who carries which end of a crate. Alexander and Laura watch them. The other Islanders continue to set up for the ceremony

Laura What are you two doing?
Cuffee Quashie, you walk backwards.
Quashie No, Cuffee, you walk backwards.
Cuffee I always walk backwards.
Quashie No, you always walk frontwards. Now it's your turn to walk backwards.
Alexander Why don't you just turn around?
Cuffee
Quashie } (*together*) Oh yeah ...

Cuffee and Quashie both turn to face away from the crate, and then try to carry it in opposite directions

Alexander (*sighing*) No, no, no. Like this.

Alexander turns Cuffee and Quashie around until they finally work it out. They carry the crate to its position for the ceremony. Fruit and vegetables can be placed on it by the other Islanders

Laura, what else do we need?
Laura I think we've got everything ... (*She looks around to check*)
Cuffee This is like a party, right, Alexander?
Alexander Yeah, sort of.
Quashie So — we were just wondering ...
Cuffee
Quashie } Is there gonna be cake?

The Islanders, with Laura and Alexander, turn to glare at them

Cuffee (*mumbling*) We were only asking ...
Quashie (*mumbling*) Yeah, I mean, we helped and everything ...

The focus switches back to Fafa or the main state lighting dips and the special on Fafa brightens. The Islanders finish their preparations for the ceremony

Sun God (*voice over*) If you don't ask me now, I'm going to tell you the answer anyway, and you hate it when I do that.
Fafa OK, OK. I know it's sort of against the rules, but I watch them down there all the time, and it's coming up to my final exams, and I haven't had any practical experience of being a god, you know, like helping them down there and all that, so ...
Sun God (*voice over*) So you want to go down there.
Fafa Yes. Can I?
Sun God (*voice over*) No.
Fafa But Dad ——
Sun God (*voice over*) Tradition says that ——
Fafa (*sighing*) Tradition.
Sun God (*voice over*) Tradition says that a god cannot appear on the island unless he is summoned by mortals. You know that.
Fafa Tradition says gods don't watch TV. Can't I go down, just this once?
Sun God (*voice over*) Tradition is our strongest connection with the island, and that's one of the lessons you should be learning for your exams. Tradition has a power all of its own ...

The focus switches back to the Island. Bring up a general, bright, full stage wash

No. 2 Prayer to the Gods

Alexander and Laura lead all the other Islanders in their ceremony to the gods. They sing

Alexander	In the green plantations of fruit so sweet ...
Islanders	See the gods who provide for us,
	The gods who provide for us.
Laura	From the highest mountains to the valleys at their feet ...
Islanders	See the gods who provide for us,
	The gods who provide for us.
Alexander **Laura** **Islanders**	Hear our voices, Raised to you to say How we thank you for each new day. Hear our voices, Raised to you to say ...

Islanders	We raise our voice today …
Alexander / **Laura**	Raise our voice today …
Islanders	Raise our voice today …
Alexander / **Laura**	Raise our voice today …
Islanders	Raise our voice to say …
Alexander / **Laura**	Raise our voice to …
Alexander / **Laura** / **Islanders**	Thank you for each new day.
Alexander	In the arms of family, the ones we love,
Islanders	Feel the gods who guide us, The gods who guide us.
Laura	Watching over us, from the skies above,
Islanders	Feel the gods who guide us, The gods who guide us.
Alexander / **Laura** / **Islanders**	Hear our voices, raised to you to say How we thank you for each new day. Hear our voices, raised to you to say …
Islanders	We raise our voice today…
Alexander / **Laura**	Raise our voice today…
Islanders	Raise our voice today…
Alexander / **Laura**	Raise our voice today…
Islanders	Raise our voice to say…
Alexander / **Laura**	Raise our voice to …
Alexander / **Laura** / **Islanders**	Thank you for each new day. Hear our voices, raised to you to say How we thank you for each new day. Hear our voices, raised to you to say ...
Islanders	We raise our voice today …
Alexander / **Laura**	Raise our voice today …
Islanders	Raise our voice today …
Alexander / **Laura**	Raise our voice today …

Islanders	Raise our voice to say …
Alexander	Raise our voice to …
Laura	
Islanders	Thank you for each new …

Thunder and lighting, and if required, cannon fire from the pirate ship

> *Suddenly, a group of Pirates, including Captain George and his First Mate, sail or run on. They wear pirate hats, swords in sword belts, etc. Captain George wears a pirate captain's hat, a hoop earring and a sword in a sword belt*

During the following, the First Mate never leaves Captain George's side

The Islanders scream. Cuffee and Quashie try to hide behind Alexander. Ol' Manbo sees the Pirates and moves away a little, as if to hide herself from them

The Lights change to a general, morning, full stage wash

Capt. George (*speaking with a "pirate" accent*) Go get 'em, lads!

The Pirates surround the Islanders, and Captain George stops in the centre next to Alexander and Laura. The Pirates menace with their swords drawn and the Islanders cower

> Having a little ceremony, eh? Not interrupting, are we? (*He laughs*)

Captain George's Pirates take his laughing as an invitation to laugh as well

Alexander Who are you?
Capt. George I am … (*He pauses for effect*)
First Mate (*interrupting*) The Famous, Ferocious, Feared, Fantastic, Fripperous — the one and only Pirate Captain George and His Terrifyingly Treacherous Band of Pirates!

The Pirates cheer

Capt. George (*dryly*) Thank you. And this is my First Mate … umm … First Mate. And from now on, we are in charge around here.

The Pirates give a small round of applause for their Captain

Laura Pirates? Don't be silly. Real pirates only exist in history books. And you look stupid in that hat.

Skool & Crossbones 9

Capt. George I do not! (*He clears his throat*) First Mate, tell them The Rules.
First Mate Yes, sir! Rule number one ...
Pirates One!
First Mate The Captain is in charge! Rule number two ...
Pirates Two!
First Mate I'm his number two! Rule number three ...
Pirates Three!
First Mate No boring church services ever, especially on Sundays! Rule number four ...
Pirates Four!
First Mate No lessons or homework ever, especially geography!

The Pirates cheer

And rule number five ...
Pirates Five!
First Mate Chocolate sauce will be served with every meal!

The Pirates cheer

Capt. George You are clearly having a bit of a church service here, and rule number two ——
First Mate Three.
Capt. George Three clearly states that church services are not allowed, especially today! (*He laughs*)

The Pirates laugh along with Captain George. He sharply indicates for them to stop and they do so immediately

Cuffee They can't just sail up here and tell us what to do!
Quashie Yeah! We have rights, you know!

All the Pirates, including Captain George and his First Mate, turn to Cuffee and Quashie and point their swords at them

Cuffee On the other hand ...
Quashie Welcome! Anything you need ——
Cuffee Just ask.
Quashie Yeah. Nice hat, by the way.
Capt. George At ease, men.
Alexander (*to Captain George*) Look, you can't just sail up to the island and take over. It ... It doesn't work that way.
Laura No, it doesn't! This isn't the seventeenth century, you know.

Capt. George Oh, we're not going to take over the island, are we, lads?
A Pirate No, Cap'n. Just the beach!
Another Pirate And the food!
A Third Pirate Don't forget the chocolate sauce!
Capt. George That's right, lads!

Captain George laughs. The Pirates laugh with him until he sharply indicates for them to stop

Laura Don't you dare ...!
Capt. George Oh, oi dares. Oi dares. Oo-argh!
Pirates Oo-argh!
First Mate And what are you gonna do about it, eh?
Alexander We'll just find — whoever brought you here, and they can just come and take you away!
Capt. George Oh, that might be a little tricky, I'm afraid. Allow us to explain. First Mate?
First Mate Yes, Cap'n George, sir?
Capt. George Prepare the crew!
First Mate Aye, aye, sir! (*He turns to the Pirate crew*) Avast, men, measure the anchor, drop the jib, tally ho, left right, left right!

The Lights change to a general, bright, full stage wash

Captain George looks questioningly at the First Mate. The First Mate shrugs and moves away. Captain George sighs with despair. The Pirates all shuffle, panic and generally fuss around until they are at last in position. The Pirates act out the story as they sing

No. 3 The Mutiny

Capt. George	'Twas a bright and breezy morning, When we left our English mooring, On the good ship Tyriania, my friend. In our classroom, not a sound, For we were seaward bound, And who knew where our travelling would end?
Pirates	Yo-ho-ho and a bottle of rum. Splice the mainsail till she's done. Pieces of eight to all will come. Yo-ho-ho — and a bottle of rum.

Skool & Crossbones

Capt. George Our headmistress was a dragon;
You would need the largest flagon
Of the strongest rum to bear her nagging tone.

On this school trip she had planned
To keep us all in hand,
But we had other plans to sail alone.

Pirates Yo-ho-ho and a bottle of eight.
Splice the anchor with a weight.
Pieces of rum and a rolling gait.
Yo-ho-ho — and a bottle of eight.

Capt. George One stormy night at sea,
When she thought that all of we
Were safely tucked below, asleep at last,
She was gazing at the ocean.
We crept up without commotion ...

The Pirates poise, one foot in the air, waiting for the command

(*Speaking*) Go get her!
(*Singing*) And captured her and tied her to the mast.

Pirates Yo-ho-ho and a bottle of bold.
Splice the eye-patch in the hold.
Doubloons young and pirates gold.
Yo-ho-ho — and a bottle of bold.

Capt. George With her screams, the crew from slumber
Did awake, but we outnumbered them,
And soon the sailors all had walked the plank.
As she stood upon the end,
I was slightly sad, my friend,
But I pushed her in and watched her 'til she sank.

Pirates Yo-ho-ho and a parrot of rum.
Splice the cutlass with your thumb.
Pieces of wooden legs, by gum.
Yo-ho-ho — and a parrot of rum.

Capt. George Well, now the tale is told
Of our mutiny so bold,
So here we stand as pirates of the sea.

                    I have told it all to you
                    So you know that this is true:
                    We'll conquer all, and all will bow to me!

Pirates   Bow to he!

Capt. George ⎱ Yo-ho-ho — and a bottle of rum.
Pirates   ⎰ They'll / We'll obey me / him, every one.
                    Till our fearsome work is done.
                    Yo-ho-ho, yo-ho-ho — and a bottle of rum.

The Lights change to a general, mid-morning, full stage wash

Captain George confronts Alexander and the Islanders again

Alexander You made your headmistress walk the plank?
Capt. George Well, it seemed like a good idea at the time.
Laura And you've been sailing around as pirates ever since?
First Mate That's right, and very fierce pirates we are too!

The Pirates all shout in agreement

Capt. George So, if you do what I say, I'm sure we can all get along just fine.
Cuffee Alexander, we can't let them get away with this!

The Islanders speak in agreement

Quashie Yeah! Someone should do something!

Everyone is quiet and looks at Quashie

   Someone who isn't me.
Alexander Captain George, you just get back on your boat and sail away, and we'll say no more about it.
Capt. George Shan't.
Laura Why not?
Capt. George We've conquered the oceans —— !
First Mate — and now we've come to conquer the land!
A Pirate Plus we ran out of chocolate sauce.

Captain George and the First Mate snarl at the Pirate. The Pirate edges away

Alexander Well, you can take some food, but you can't just stay here and order us around. Right, everyone?
Islanders Right/ Yeah/No, he can't/You tell him, Alexander... (*Etc. ad lib*)
First Mate You dare to defy the Famous, Ferocious, Feared, Fantastic, Fripperous ...!
Capt. George (*quietening the First Mate*) All right, all right, First Mate. I think they get the idea. (*To the Islanders*) I'll give you until sunset, and then if you're not ready to surrender — it will be sword fights until dawn! (*He laughs maniacally*)

The other Pirates all laugh loudly. Captain George stops laughing and turns to glare at the Pirates, causing them to stop

Back to the Tyriania, men!

All the Pirates move towards the exit. Captain George and the First Mate follow

(*To the First Mate; in a non-pirate, very posh accent*) Look, they don't have to laugh every time I laugh. Sometimes, it's more scary if I laugh and the rest of you menace, do you see?

The Pirates, Captain George and the First Mate exit

Quashie Well, I wasn't scared of them.
Cuffee Me neither.
Quashie Yes, you were! You hid behind Alexander!
Cuffee That was a tactic. Anyway, you hid too!
Quashie I had a plan!
Alexander Give it a rest. (*To Laura*) What are we going to do?
Quashie We could fight them!
Islanders Yeah! / Let's fight them / Alexander! / Sword-fights till dawn! (*Etc. ad lib*)

Cuffee jumps onto a crate. He takes a banana from his pocket and wields it like a sword

Cuffee I could face the Pirate Captain with my sword held up high, and save the day with a thrust and a parry and a thrust and ...

Cuffee gets a bit carried away and falls off the box, knocking Quashie over in the process. Everyone laughs

Laura That's all very well, Cuffee, but fighting isn't the answer. Anyway, we don't have any swords, and they've been learning how to be pirates since they took over the ship.
Alexander She's got a point.
Islanders Yeah, she has. / What are we going to do? / Well, I think we could fight them ... (*Etc. ad lib*)
Ol' Manbo (*looking up from her book*) Pirate: noun. One who robs at sea; marauder, buccaneer. The real ones were very fierce, oh yes, very fierce indeed.
Cuffee What did she say?
Quashie Who?
Cuffee Ol' Manbo.
Ol' Manbo You can't fight them. Look at you. Hopeless, all of you. You might as well ask the god of the sun to come down here and sort this out for you. There's as much chance of that happening as there is of you winning a fight against them. Hopeless.

Ol' Manbo disappears into her hut

Alexander Well. That was helpful. Anyone else got a good idea?
Laura She might be right, actually.
Cuffee About us being hopeless?
Quashie You're hopeless.
Cuffee No, you're hopeless.
Laura She might be right about the Sun God.
Alexander Yeah, there hasn't been a summoning since your grandmother used to do them.
Laura No, I mean — we could try it.
Cuffee Summon him?
Islanders Summon him? / Down to the island? / Wow, cool ... (*Etc. ad lib*)
Quashie You mean, so he appears? Real? Here?
Laura Well, today is his day.
Alexander (*to Laura*) Do you know how to do that?
Laura I think so. I've heard my grandmother talk about it often enough.
Alexander Umm ... Maybe we should stand well back.
Laura No, no. You have to join in. It only works if we all do it together. I just need to remember the words ...

The focus returns to Fafa or the main state lighting dips and a special comes up

Fafa Dad! Dad, they're ...!
Sun God (*voice over*) I hate to sound like a know-it-all, but ...
Fafa You knew this was going to happen.

Skool & Crossbones

Sun God (*voice over*) Yep.
Fafa Well? Are you …?
Sun God (*voice over*) Going down there? I should, but there's a really good spy movie on …
Fafa So …?
Sun God (*voice over*; *sighing*) OK. You can go down there …
Fafa Yes!
Sun God (*voice over*) On one condition.
Fafa Anything!
Sun God (*voice over*) No magic.
Fafa What?! But how can I practise being a god if I can't …
Sun God (*voice over*) You can practise being mortal. It'll be good research, and I'll keep an eye on you.
Fafa OK. Can I go now?
Sun God (*voice over*) You have to wait for the right moment. It's trad——
Fafa (*interrupting*) Traditional. I know, I know.

Fafa exits

The focus returns to the Island, or cut special and brighten main state lighting

Ol' Manbo enters and watches the song

No. 4. The Summoning of Fafa (chant)

Laura (*to herself*) Nous en appelons aux dieux. (*To the others*) Nous en appelons aux dieux.

Laura claps a rhythm and the Islanders repeat after her. The clapping builds into counter-rhythms. When this is established, they begin to dance around the pattern and chant over the rhythms

| **Islanders** | Nous en appelons aux dieux. |
| | Nous en appelons aux dieux. |

| **Alexander** **Laura** **Cuffee** **Quashie** | Fafa, warrior god, Hear our chant and hear my plea. Fafa, warrior god, We call on you to set us free. | **Islanders** Nous en appelons aux dieux. Nous en appelons aux dieux. Nous en appelons aux dieux. Nous en appelons aux dieux. |

Alexander **Laura** **Cuffee** **Quashie**	Fafa, god of fire Instill our hearts with courage true. Fafa, god of fire In times of fear we look to you.	**Islanders** Nous en appelons aux dieux. Nous en appelons aux dieux. Nous en appelons aux dieux. Nous en appelons aux dieux.
All	Nous en appelons aux dieux. Nous en appelons aux dieux. Nous en appelons aux dieux. Nous en appelons aux dieux. Fafa!	

Thunder and lightning, and a cloud of smoke (optional). The Islanders scream and back off. The smoke begins to clear

Fafa appears within the clearing smoke. He shakes his head, steadies himself and looks around

Restore general, bright, mid-morning, full stage wash lighting

Cuffee **Quashie** } (*together*) Wow!
Laura I didn't think it would actually work.
Fafa Whoo! That was fun! Oh. Hello! I'm Fafa.
Cuffee No, you're not!
Alexander Cuffee!
Quashie But Alexander, he can't be the god of the sun! He's smaller than me!
Laura Quashie, don't be rude!
Fafa Sorry, I should explain. I'm Fafa, son of Fafa.
Cuffee Do you know who we are?
Quashie Of course he doesn't. The gods don't have time to learn everybody's name …
Fafa Hey, Cuffee, Quashie. Nice to meet you, Alexander, Laura. Hey everyone. So, you guys are having some trouble with pirates?
Islanders (*overlapping*) The pirates are taking over our island / There's these pirates, and they're horrible / Captain George and his pirates are going to fight us tonight … (*Etc. ad lib*)
Alexander Guys!

Everyone is quiet

(*Turning to Fafa*) We've been invaded by pirates, and they've given us till sunset to surrender, or we have to fight them. We need some help. No offence, but are you sure you're up to it?
Fafa Of course I am!

Ol' Manbo moves forwards to get a good look at Fafa. She laughs out loud

Ol' Manbo You really think he's a god, don't you? You think you clapped your hands and said a few stupid words and summoned a god!
Fafa Hey!
Alexander Yeah, thanks, Ol' Manbo.
Laura Sorry about her. She's a bit — weird.
Ol' Manbo Weird?! I'm not the one who thinks that is a god!
Fafa I am a god!
Ol' Manbo Prove it!
Fafa I will!
Ol' Manbo How?
Fafa I'll use magic to turn you into a …

Thunder and lighting

Oh.
Ol' Manbo You can't use magic. You're hopeless, just like the rest of them.
Cuffee Go on, use magic!
Quashie Yeah! Can you turn Cuffee into a frog?
Cuffee Hey!
Ol' Manbo No discipline around here, that's the trouble. Hopeless.

Ol' Manbo turns and goes back into her hut

Fafa Look, we don't need magic — or her. We'll fight the pirates and beat them at their own game. Get your swords, and we'll ——
Quashie (*interrupting*) We don't have any swords.
Fafa Oh. Well, who has got swords?
Islanders (*pointing towards the direction of the Pirates' ship*) They have!
Fafa Then we'll take theirs!
Laura How can we take theirs?
Fafa We'll distract them so we can creep on to the ship. Watch this. (*He strolls up to the ship or calls off stage if the production does not use a ship*) Ahoy there, aboard the Tyriania!

Captain George enters, followed by the First Mate. The other Pirates enter gradually

Capt. George Who's doing all that shouting?
Fafa Me!
Capt. George Who's me?
Alexander He's ... um ... my cousin — Oswald!
Capt. George Oswald?

Captain George laughs and the Pirates laugh too. Fafa turns to Alexander and gives him a questioning look. Alexander shrugs at him

First Mate Ah-ha! So, Cousin Oswald, finally you surrender to the power of the Famous, Ferocious, Feared ...

Captain George glares at the First Mate

Capt. George Will you stop doing my line!
First Mate Sorry, Cap'n.
Fafa We've been thinking, Captain, sir, that you must be very fierce pirates indeed.
Capt. George Oh we are that, aren't we lads, eh?
First Mate Aren't we, lads?
Pirates Yes, we are / oo-ar, oo-ar, oo-ar, etc. (*One or two growl*)
Fafa And you must have learnt a lot about piracy from the history books ...
Capt. George 'Tis a fine and distinguished history, my friend. I could tell you a tale or two about our predecessors ...
Fafa Oh, please do.
Islanders Yes, please / We'd love to hear / Tell us about pirates ... (*Etc. ad lib*)
Capt. George How 'bout it, lads?
A Pirate I love a good story, me!
Another Pirate Nothing like a good story to get you ready for a fight!
A Third Pirate Let's tell 'em, Cap'n!
Fafa (*aside to Alexander*) Now's your chance! While they tell us the story, send someone on to the ship to steal swords!
Capt. George Let the tales begin!

The Lights change to a general, bright, full stage wash

During the song, Cuffee and Quashie sneak on to the ship or off stage and return to shore carrying a large, old trunk

Some or all the pirates including Captain George and his First Mate divide in three singing groups for the following song

No. 5 A Pirate History

All Pirates The history of piracy
Is full of blood and fear.
You can sing along,
If your stomach's strong
And join us as we cheer.

Oh, the life of a pirate is a noble life!
Awash with rum and full of strife!

There's treasure galore
And more in store ...
Yes the life of a pirate is a fine and noble life!

Pirate Group 1 L'Ollonais the Frenchman was
A cruel buccaneer.
He'd cut your heart out with a knife
And dunk it in his beer.

All Pirates Eurgh!

Pirate Group 1 He was captured by some natives and
His end was rather grim.
They roasted him upon a spit
And tore him limb from limb.

All Pirates They roasted him upon a spit
And tore him limb from limb!

Oh, the life of a pirate is a noble life!
Awash with rum and full of strife!

Pirate Group 1 They'll eat you hot
Or let you rot!
All Pirates Yes the life of a pirate is a fine and noble life!

Pirate Group 2 Blackbeard was the King all right,
The fiercest of the lot.
His beard was lit with fuses
So his chin was rather hot!

All Pirates Ow!

Pirate Group 2 It took them twenty cutlass wounds
To kill the mean old goat.
When he was dead, they hung his head
On the bowsprit of the boat!

All Pirates When he was dead, they hung his head
On the bowsprit of the boat!

Oh, the life of a pirate is a noble life!
Awash with rum and full of strife!

Pirate Group 2 Just light your beard
And you'll be feared!

All Pirates Yes the life of a pirate is a fine and noble life!

Pirate Group 3 Sweet Mary Read was a lovely lass
But when her husband died,
She left her home and bought a ship.
A Pirate's life she tried.

All Pirates Ooo!

Pirate Group 3 Anne Bonny travelled with her, and
They shot men full of holes.
When merchants saw the ship approach,
They cried, "Lord, save our souls!"

All Pirates When merchants saw the ship approach
They cried, "Lord, save our souls!"

Oh, the life of a pirate is a noble life!
Awash with rum and full of strife!

Pirate Group 3 The women too!
They'll run you through!

All Pirates Yes the life of a pirate is a fine and noble life!
The life of a pirate is a fine and noble ...
Fine and noble life!

The Pirates laugh heartily and congratulate each other

Capt. George Right lads! Back to the ship! And we'll see you at sunset!

Music underscore (No.5a Exit of Pirates)

The Lights change to a general, afternoon, full stage wash

> *The Captain and his crew disappear back on to the ship or off stage*

> *Ol' Manbo enters from her hut and watches the Islanders*

Cuffee and Quashie bring out the trunk they took from the ship, and Fafa opens it up

Fafa Right, what did we get?
Alexander Well, we didn't get swords … (*He starts to hand out various kitchen implements: wooden spoons, egg whisks etc. from the trunk*)
Laura But we could bake them a cake.
Cuffee \
Quashie / (*together*) Cake?!
Fafa Hey, this is easy! I can just use magic to turn these into …

Thunder and lightning

OK. Maybe magic isn't a good idea.
Cuffee Can you actually do any magic?
Quashie Card tricks? Sawing people in half?
Laura Stop it, you two. Look, at least we've got some eyepatches. (*She pulls two eyepatches out of the trunk and tries one on for size*)
Fafa Essential for the best pirate.
Quashie And — a — trumpet? (*He pulls a sink plunger out of the trunk*)
Alexander (*sighing*) That's a plunger, you idiot.
Cuffee (*pulling a parrot out of the trunk*) And a parrot! It doesn't look very happy though …
Laura (*examining the parrot*) That's because it's dead.
Cuffee No, it's not! It's just — asleep.
Quashie Resting.
Alexander Deceased.
Fafa Stuffed.
Cuffee Oh. Oh well, at least it won't need feeding! (*He holds the parrot on his shoulder*) How does it look?
Alex \
Fafa \
Laura / (*together*) Dead.
Quashie /

Laura reaches into the trunk and pulls out a beach ball

Laura OK, who took this?

Quashie holds up his hand excitedly, and then realizes that everyone is looking rather crossly at him

Quashie *(sheepishly)* I thought we could have a game later ...
Ol' Manbo Hopeless.
Alexander Just ignore her. It's nearly evening, and we've got to be ready by sunset. Come on, you lot. Let's see if we can find anything else to use instead of swords.

The Islanders all exit slowly, chatting

Fafa stands to one side and talks to Alexander and Laura. Meanwhile, Cuffee throws the parrot into the trunk, slams the lid shut and starts to walk away. Quashie, standing by the trunk, makes a screeching parrot sound. Cuffee runs back to the trunk and opens it quickly. Quashie bursts out laughing. Cuffee glares at him and closes the lid

Quashie and Cuffee carry the trunk off and exit. Alexander and Laura exit

Fafa makes to follow Alexander and Laura

Ol' Manbo *(calling Fafa back)* You, boy. I want to talk to you.
Fafa What about?
Ol' Manbo Don't be rude. And stand up straight when I'm talking to you.
Fafa You can't talk to me like that! I'm a god!
Ol' Manbo Of course you are. And I'm the Queen of England. Now, about these so-called pirates. What are you waiting for? Just attack them and be done with it so we can have some peace and quiet around here.
Fafa Attack them with what? Wooden spoons and cheese graters? I came down here to help and so far all I've done is make them look stupid.
Ol' Manbo Oh, stop whining. Pull yourself together and fight like a man!
Fafa Hey, whose side are you on, anyway?
Ol' Manbo My own. Now stop messing around and do the work you came to do!
Fafa You sound like my dad.

The Islanders with Alexander, Laura, Cuffee and Quashie, come running back on to the stage. They are all dressed in things they took from the Pirates, including various improvised bits and pieces and kitchen utensils. They use the kitchen utensils as swords and are very clumsy with them. They look like a bunch of misfit, second-hand pirates: nothing fits them very well

Skool & Crossbones

Alexander Come on then! Line up, everyone! Hurry up, Quashie!

They all move into a haphazard line

Right. How do we look?
Ol' Manbo Ridiculous! Just get on with the fighting, will you? Some of us haven't got all day, you know.

Ol' Manbo goes back into her hut

Laura She's right, we do look ridiculous, and we'll lose. I still say fighting's not the answer.
Cuffee We need a secret weapon …
Quashie Or some magic …
Fafa Look, my dad said I could come down here on one condition — no magic.
Alexander Can't he do some magic?
Fafa He's too busy watching a spy movie … A spy movie!
Laura We don't have time to watch TV now.
Fafa No, I'm talking about infiltration! We need to put the fear of the gods into those Pirates. Let's send some — spies!
Cuffee
Quashie } *(together; excitedly)* Spies!

Cuffee and Quashie sing the melody of the following song, No.6 The Spies, and mime being pirate spies

Fafa And it looks like we've got two volunteers. The rest of you should go off and practise your sword-fighting. It's getting close to sunset, and we need to be ready to fight the Pirates.

The Islanders exit

Cuffee This isn't gonna be dangerous, is it?
Fafa
Alexander } *(together; shaking their heads and clearly lying)* No …
Laura
Quashie And nothing's gonna happen to us, is it?
Fafa
Alexander } *(together; shaking their heads and clearly lying)* No …
Laura
Cuffee
Quashie } *(together)* Are you sure?

Fafa
Alexander   *(together; nodding a lot and blatantly lying)* Yes …
Laura
Cuffee OK.
Quashie OK.
Fafa Now to prepare — the spies!

The general stage wash dims and two open-white searchlights sweep the stage

During the song, Laura hands Cuffee and Quashie the two eyepatches and they put them on

No. 6. The Spies

Fafa   Beguiling, mysterious,
Alexander   Secretive and sly.
Laura   Alluring, brave and daring
Cuffee   Is the lifestyle of a spy.
Quashie

                 Intrigue, deceit,
                 A calculated lie.
                 Exciting and adventurous:
                 The lifestyle of a spy!

During a musical break they all mime being spies

Fafa   On to the ship you ease,
                 Soft as a summer breeze.
Alexander   Cool and clever, you
                 Know just what to do.
Laura   Soon you'll hear
                 Pirates near!

Cuffee   We will find a way
Quashie   We can hide away,
                 Then we'll listen to
                 Everything they do.

Cuffee   Secret spies …
Quashie   Secret spies …
Cuffee   In disguise.
Quashie

Skool & Crossbones

Fafa **Alexander** **Laura**	Danger Unmentionable. The risk is very high. Villains Undetentionable: The target of the spy.
Cuffee **Quashie**	(*speaking; together*) Danger? I think I heard someone call my name ...
Fafa **Alexander** **Laura**	(*speaking; together*) Too late! You volunteered to play the spying game!

During a musical interlude Cuffee and Quashie try to escape but the others stop them

Fafa (*singing*)	Do what you have to do. We'll all be watching you.
Alexander	Stay in your hiding place. Don't let them see your face.
Laura	We'll be here, Always near.
Cuffee **Quashie**	I guess we have to go On to the ship, although We'd rather stay right here. Let's make that very clear.
Fafa **Alexander** **Laura** **Cuffee** **Quashie**	Now it's time. You / we must climb...
Fafa **Alexander** **Laura**	In the disguise —— In the disguise ——
Cuffee **Quashie**	In the disguise ——
Fafa **Alexander** **Laura** **Cuffee** **Quashie**	—— of spies!

Music underscore (No. 6a Scene Change Music)

   Fafa, Alexander and Laura exit

Cuffee and Quashie hide

   The Pirates with Captain George and his First Mate come down from the ship or enter from the wings. Captain George sits on one of the crates

Cuffee and Quashie slip out from their hiding place to mingle with the Pirates

It is evening, and a storm is brewing over the island. Thunder and lightning are seen and heard in the distance

   Capt. George We'll have fun defeating these puny islanders, won't we lads?
   First Mate Won't we, lads?
   Pirates Oo-ar / Aye, Captain, that we will / Nothing like a good sword-fight / Victory will be ours! *(Etc. ad lib)*

   The Pirates laugh

Scaredy-Cat, one of the Pirates, looks nervous and stands slightly apart from the others in the shadows. Cuffee and Quashie approach. Scaredy-Cat, doesn't recognize that Cuffee and Quashie are strangers

   Scaredy-Cat I don't like this place at all. It's scary. I'd much rather be back at school.
   Cuffee Umm — me too. I mean, what if the gods they worship here are real?
   Quashie They wouldn't be very happy about us attacking the island, would they?
   Cuffee That's right. They might even do some — magic ...
   Quashie And turn us all into giant frogs ...
   Scaredy-Cat Giant frogs?
   Cuffee Or send a plague of slimy snakes ...
   Scaredy-Cat Slimy snakes?
   Quashie Oh yes. Or they might just send down a bolt of lightning and (*he makes the sound of a lightning bolt strike and then mimes being hit by it*) nothing but a pile of ashes.
   Scaredy-Cat A pile of ashes? Do you think their gods would really do that?
   Cuffee I dunno. Pretty stormy sky tonight.
   Quashie Ask the Captain. He'll know.
   Scaredy-Cat Right.

Scaredy-Cat makes his way nervously over towards where Captain George is sitting, but not too close

   Umm — Captain, sir?

Capt. George Speak up, lad!
Scaredy-Cat Well, sir, I was just wondering — what do we do if they summon one of their gods to help them, sir?

All the Pirates laugh, including Captain George and his First Mate

First Mate Don't be bothering the Captain with such ridiculous notions!

Captain George stands slowly and walks nonchalantly over to Scaredy-Cat

Capt. George The gods, eh? Does that — scare you!?

Scaredy-Cat jumps and everyone laughs at him

Scaredy-Cat Well, sir, you never know what magical powers they might have, sir.

All the Pirates stop laughing as the First Mate continues laughing very loudly

Capt. George (*pretending to be serious*) Now, now, First Mate. We mustn't laugh. I mean — who knows what lurks out there?

The Pirates begin to look a little worried

Thunder and lightning. The Lights change to a dark blue, shadowy, full stage cover

No. 7 Mumbo Jumbo

Pirates	Mumbo Jumbo Mumbo Jumbo
Scaredy-Cat	On a cold, dark night when the sea is black And the wind howls in the sail, There are times you could almost swear That there's something, someone there.
Pirates	Mumbo Jumbo Mumbo Jumbo
First Mate	You can feel their eyes burning in your back And you hear a ghostly wail. There are times you'll stop and stare To be sure there's no-one there.

Pirates	Mumbo Jumbo Mumbo Jumbo
Cuffee **Quashie**	The shadows wrap around you, like a shroud. The trembling moon has crept behind a cloud.
Pirates	Mumbo Jumbo Haunting and bizarre Hocus Pocus chanting from afar As if they think the gods will wake, The sky will fall, the earth will quake And then they'll rise before our eyes. Who do they think they are?

They all laugh until interrupted by thunder and lightning. Everyone jumps

	Mumbo Jumbo Mumbo Jumbo
Scaredy-Cat	You find yourself all alone one night When you're watching from the nest, And you hear them call to you. Then what do you do?
Pirates	Mumbo Jumbo Mumbo Jumbo
First Mate	You have no strength with which to fight, And they will never rest. Your heart is beating fast. Each breath could be your last.
Pirates	Mumbo Jumbo Mumbo Jumbo
Cuffee **Quashie**	Your fear will satisfy them for a while, But do not break the silence with a smile!
Pirates	Mumbo Jumbo Haunting and bizarre Hocus Pocus chanting from afar As if they think the gods will wake,

>   The sky will fall, the earth will quake
>   And then they'll rise before our eyes.
>   Who do they think they are?

Thunder and lightning. As this happens, the Captain jumps out at the Pirates and scares them. The Pirates all scream, and the Captain laughs

Pirates   Mumbo Jumbo
                   Mumbo Jumbo

Scaredy-Cat   You reach into your bag one night
                   And feel a great big lump.
                   Shivering, you dare
                   To peek and see what's there!

Pirates   Mumbo Jumbo,
                   Mumbo Jumbo...

First Mate   You look into the bag with fright,
                   As your heart begins to thump.
                   You shiver and you quake,
                   As your hand pulls out a snake!

Pirates   Mumbo Jumbo,
                   Mumbo Jumbo ...

Cuffee   They'll find you anywhere, you cannot hide.
Quashie   They're nasty and they're vile, it cannot be denied, oh ...

Pirates   Mumbo Jumbo
                   Haunting and bizarre
                   Hocus Pocus chanting from afar
                   As if they think the gods will wake,
                   The sky will fall, the earth will quake
                   And then they'll rise before our eyes.
                   Who do they think they are?

                   Mumbo Jumbo, Mumbo Jumbo
                   Mumbo Jumbo, Mumbo Jumbo
                   Mumbo Jumbo, Mumbo Jumbo
                   Mumbo Jumbo, Mumbo Jumbo

Thunder and lightning, much louder and lighter than the first two bursts. Everyone screams. The Lights change to general, night time, full stage wash

Scaredy-Cat It's the gods! They're going to turn us into giant frogs!
Cuffee Quick! Run back to the ship!
Quashie Sail away, before it's too late!

The Pirates run around in a panic, trying to get past each other and back to the ship. Captain George stands in the middle of them, and catches Cuffee and Quashie as they run past

Pirates Back to the ship! / Get out of my way! / I don't want to be a giant frog! (*Etc. ad lib*)
Capt. George Calm down, look, just stop, First Mate, everyone ... Atten — tion!

The Pirates freeze and come to attention

Right. Now then, who have we here?
First Mate Intruders, sir!
Capt. George Enemy spies, eh?
Cuffee No, no, we're pirates ...
Quashie Yes, yes, we're pirates ...
Cuffee
Quashie } (*together*) Oo. Ar.
Capt. George Right then, tell me, how do you feel about — geography?
Cuffee It's really cool, you get to learn about clouds and read maps ——
Quashie — and find out about interesting places, and ——
Pirates Intruders!
Capt. George I knew it! We're taking you hostage! Tie these spies up with a couple of good knots, lads!
First Mate Aye, aye, Cap'n!

The First Mate and some Pirates take Cuffee and Quashie to the ship and tie them to the mast. If the ship is not visible on stage they can be tied to a tree or to each other

Cuffee Alexander!
Quashie Laura!
Cuffee
Quashie } (*together*) Fafa! Help!

Alexander, Laura, Fafa and the Islanders race onstage. Ol' Manbo comes out of her hut and watches the action

Laura You let them go!

Capt. George Shan't!
Alexander You're going to pay for this!
Capt. George Oh yeah? How much?
Fafa Let them go or I'll turn you into a ...

Thunder and lightning

> But, Dad ...!

Thunder and lightning

Capt. George Where are the gods when you need them, eh? (*He laughs*)

The Pirates laugh with Captain George

Fafa That's enough! Prepare for battle, Captain George!
Capt. George It will be my pleasure. First Mate?! Prepare for battle!
First Mate Aye, Cap'n! Pirates! Prepare to fight!
Fafa Alexander — hand me that flag!

Thunder and lightning. White lighting comes up from the footlights

The Pirates line up in formation behind the Captain. One of them hands him the skull and crossbones flag from the pirate ship. The Islanders draw their weapons and stand behind Fafa. Alexander hands Fafa the flag with the bright yellow sun on a bright orange background

Fafa sings to the skies

No. 8. Tonight We Fight!

Fafa   I call up to the gods,
For into battle we must go
To fight against the odds
And beat the pirate foe.

Prepare yourselves, my friends,
With courage and with pride,
To fight until the end.
The gods are on our side.

Capt. George 'Tis almost sunset! Take up your swords, me hearties, and prepare to conquer this island!

The Pirates cheer

> Now the battling starts. We'll cut out their hearts.
> There's nothing like fighting for fun.
> And amid the commotion beside the blue ocean,
> I have a small notion that they'll be outdone.
>
> With our swords held on high, we'll utter the cry,
> "Face us and fight us or run!"
> Then we'll slice them in two, or capture a few,
> And I fear that this battle is easily won.

First Mate	They're gonna need the strength of the gods!
Alexander	We'll beat them against all odds!
All	Tonight we fight!
Islanders	Fight for our right to be free …
Pirates	To conquer the land and the sea …
Islanders	Tonight…
All	We fight!
Islanders	This island is ours.
Pirates	Their magical pow'rs are no threat.
All	We'll attack when the sun has set.

Fafa
Alexander
Laura We'll show the Pirate Captain
Cuffee That we're not afraid.
Quashie They'll wish with all their hearts,
That to the gods they'd prayed!

Fafa   **Islanders**
Alexander We'll show the   Captain George will
Laura   Pirate Captain
Cuffee   That we're not afraid.   Be afraid.
Quashie   They'll wish with all   To the gods
                 their hearts
               That to the gods they'd They should have prayed.
                 prayed!

Capt. George
First Mate When, without hesitation or use of libation,
Three Pirates Our sea occupation succeeds upon land,
We'll live by the vow that we never shall bow
To the gods they believe are at hand.

Skool & Crossbones

| **Capt. George**
First Mate
Three Pirates | When, without
   hesitation or use of libation,
Our sea occupation
   succeeds upon land,
We'll live by the vow
   that we never shall bow
To the gods they believe are
   at hand. | **Pirates**
We will

Win onland.

No gods

Are at hand. |

Fafa/ Alexander **Laura/ Cuffee** **Quashie**	**Islanders**	**Capt. George/** **First Mate/** **Three Pirates/**	**Pirates**

We'll show the
  Pirate Captain
That we're not
  afraid.
They'll wish with
  all their hearts
That to the gods
  they'd prayed.
	Captain George
	  will
	Be afraid.
	
	To the gods
	
	They should
	  have prayed.
		When, without
		  hesitation or
		  use of libation,
		Our sea occupation
		  succeeds upon land,
		We'll live by the vow
		  that we never shall
		  bow
		To the gods they
		  believe are at hand.
			We will
			
			Win onland.
			
			No gods
			
			Are at hand.

Capt. George	Their merciful pleas we'll ignore!
Fafa	We'll plead them for mercy no more!
All	For tonight we fight!
Islanders	Fight for our right to be free!
Pirates	To conquer the land and the sea …
Islanders	Tonight …
All	We fight!
Islanders	Defending our home, With all of our might!
Pirates	We'll show them our bark's Not as bad as our bite!
Islanders	We'll force them to leave …
Pirates	There'll be no reprieve
All	For tonight — we fight! We fight!
(*Shouting*)	Tonight!

The fight begins

Ol' Manbo comes out of her hut to watch

The battle is fierce. One by one all of the Islanders, including Laura and Alexander, are captured by the Pirates. By the time the battle ends Fafa is the only one that remains standing on the Islanders' side. He surveys the scene. The Pirates have various injuries, one has a plunger as a wooden leg, another Pirate wears an eyepatch and a third Pirate has a bandage on his knee. Captain George steps forward to speak to Fafa

Music underscore (No. 8a Dialogue)

Capt. George As you are the last, you have the privilege of facing the Captain himself!
Ol' Manbo (*laughing*) Watch out for that one! He says he's a god!
Capt. George Who's she?
Fafa Ol' Manbo, stay out of this!
Capt. George Need help from an old woman, do we? She'd probably fight better than you lot!

The Pirates laugh

Come on then, old woman. I'll fight you for the island!
Ol' Manbo Just be careful what you wish for, young man.

Captain George laughs, and the rest of the pirates laugh with him. He gestures for them to stop. Fafa pulls himself up to his very tallest height

Fafa Captain George, listen carefully. I am Fafa, son of Fafa, god of the sun! I have magical powers, and you cannot defeat me!

Thunder and lightning

First Mate (*laughing*) Magical powers!
Pirate Teach him a lesson, Captain!
Another Pirate Yeah, show him the power of your sword, Captain!
Fafa If you take one step closer, I'll ... I'll ... I'll summon the most terrifying demon you have ever dreamt of!

Music underscore ends. Thunder and lightning

Capt. George One step closer, eh?

Captain George makes two false moves towards Fafa, and then takes one very slow, deliberate step towards him

Fafa Right! Don't say I didn't warn you! (*He makes gestures in the air and gradually moves around Captain George in a circle as he chants. The actor can invent his own gibberish chant and the more ridiculous it sounds, the better. It should end with a loud and clear "Boo!"*)

Thunder rumbles are heard overhead

A pause. Silence

Music underscore (No. 8b Ol' Manbo's Transformation begins)

Ol' Manbo stands very slowly and begins to shake. She is pulled mysteriously back into her little hut

The music starts to crescendo. The hut begins to shake and smoke pours out of the door (optional)

With Captain George in front, everybody moves closer to the door of the hut. All their knees knock together as they wait to see who or what will emerge from the hut. The music reaches its climax

Ol' Manbo enters, dressed as the Headmistress, complete with a mortar board, a gown, a pair of horn-rimmed spectacles and a whistle on a string around her neck

Pirates Headmistress!

The Lights change to a general, bright, full stage wash

The Pirates, except Captain George, immediately let their captives go, and rush to line up in height order for inspection. Captain George stands in shock and cannot move

Fafa Did you see that? It worked! Thanks, Dad!
Alexander Ol' Manbo?
Laura Is that you?
Headmistress It is indeed. I have been waiting for this moment for a whole year.
Alexander But — who are you?

The Headmistress walks slowly to Captain George and takes hold of his ear

Headmistress Yes, George Lancefield-Harris, Head Boy of St John's School. Who am I, exactly?

Capt. George Umm ... You're our Headmistress, miss.
Headmistress Precisely. The Headmistress that you ——?
Capt. George Umm — pushed overboard, miss?
Headmistress Exactly. And now you are all in ——?
Capt. George Trouble, miss?
Headmistress Correct. Now take off that ridiculous hat. And as Head Boy, you know perfectly well that earrings are not permitted.
Capt. George Sorry. (*He takes off his captain's hat and earring, and hands them to the First Mate*)

The First Mate also takes off his hat and throws everything over his shoulder. During the following Captain George fidgets nervously

Laura But how did you get to the island?
Headmistress I am the holder of the Teacher's Association Long Distance and Stamina Swimming Award. I simply held my breath and swam underwater until I was out of sight, and then came to the nearest island. George, don't do that.
Alexander Why didn't you tell us what had happened as soon as you got here?
Headmistress I knew that these ruffians would get tired of sailing and come ashore soon enough, so I bided my time on the island. Of course, I had to wear a disguise, in case word reached them that I was here waiting for them. That would never have done, would it, boy?
Capt. George Yes, miss. I mean, no, miss.
Fafa So why didn't you tell them who you were as soon as they landed?!
Headmistress Because I wanted to see them defeated! I wanted to see you puny islanders show some spirit for a change! Clearly, since you have never been to a proper school ...
Cuffee Hey! We go to school!
Quashie We like school!
Headmistress You like school. And that is half the problem.

The Headmistress walks down the line of Pirates. She is still holding on to Captain George's ear and he is, therefore, dragged along with her. She stops at each of the three Pirates that have the wooden leg, the eyepatch and knee bandage. During the exchange, the Islanders talk amongst themselves

Brett, stand up straight. I will take that wooden leg, thank you. Jones, are eyepatches a part of the school uniform?
A Pirate No, miss, but ...
Headmistress I thought not. Take it off at once, please. Harrison, are you injured?

Another Pirate No, Miss, but ...
Headmistress No buts. Take that bandage off immediately. What would Matron say? (*She reaches the end of the line*) Now then, I should march you all back onto the ship and sail you straight back to school.
Pirates No, miss! / Not school, miss! / Do we have to, miss? (*Etc. ad lib*)
Headmistress Silence!

The Pirates continue with their cries. The Headmistress blows her whistle loudly. The Pirates are instantly silent

However, we will not be returning to England ...

The Pirates cheer. The Islanders groan

When I arrived on the island last year, I wrote letters to all of your parents, telling them that I would be opening a new branch of the school here ...
Islanders ⎤ (*together*) What?/They're staying?/We're staying here?/
Pirates ⎦ Do you think we have to go to school with them now?/ Oh no ... (*Etc. ad lib*)
Headmistress As you will all be attending lessons together, I suggest that you make friends with each other.

Alexander offers Captain George a handshake

Alexander Friends?

Captain George scowls at him. The Headmistress gives Captain George's ear a stern tug. Captain George slaps Alexander's hand quickly with one of his, in a half-hearted handshake

Headmistress George, do it properly, please.

Captain George, still scowling, shakes Alexander's hand for half a second

George!

Captain George sighs and shakes Alexander's hand properly. Ol' Manbo nods her approval

During the following the Headmistress walks along the line of Pirates talking to them. As she does, Alexander and Laura approach Captain George and pull him to one side

Alexander We can't let her do this!
Laura (*to Captain George*) Can't you stop her?
Capt. George I pushed her off a boat! What else do you want me to do?!
Fafa Maybe I can do something. Hold on. (*Calling up to the skies*) Dad?
Sun God (*voice over*) Yes, son?
Ol' Manbo Who was that?
Cuffee His father. The god of the sun.
Quashie Ner ner nee ner ner.
Ol' Manbo Don't be ridiculous, boy. There is no god of the sun ...
Sun God (*voice over*) What did she say?!

Headmistress There will be lessons and church services every day—plenty of homework, and lots of Latin lessons for everyone. You will wear a smart gray uniform at all times — and there will be no playing games on the beach...

Thunder and lightning

Fafa Oh, now there's gonna be trouble.
Ol' Manbo Who's doing that?
Capt. George It's really him, isn't it?
Fafa Yep.
Capt. George Um, god of the sun, sir — can you please do something about her?
Fafa Dad, can I do it?
Sun God (*voice over*) Very well, son.

Music underscore (No. 8c Ol' Manbo's Transformation II)

Fafa chants. The actor can invent his own gibberish chant. It should end with a loud and clear "Boo!". Everybody else circles around the Headmistress

During the following, when the Headmistress is completely hidden from view, she takes off her gown and mortar board and puts on a fruit head-dress, á la Carmen Miranda

Headmistress Stop that ridiculous chanting this minute. Stop it, I say! What ... What are you doing? Get away from me, all of you! Get away! No! Someone help me ...!

Thunder and lightning. Everyone moves apart to reveal the Headmistress wearing the head-dress

Fafa See? Now she's got some island rhythm.

Everyone cheers

Headmistress I feel like ... like — dancing!
Sun God (*voice over*) A-one, a-two, a-one, two, three, four ...

A rhythm begins. The Headmistress starts to dance slowly. In the introduction to the number she gets quite carried away. Everyone dances with her as they sing

The Lights change to colourful carnival lighting

No. 9 Calypso Carnival

Headmistress (*Gasp!*)
(*Gasp!*)
Ow! Ow! Ow!

All Hear the rhythm, feel the beat,
Try to move your feet.
Hear the rhythm, feel the beat
Try to move your feet.
Hear the rhythm, feel the beat
Try to move your feet.
Hear the rhythm, feel the beat
Try to move your feet.

Headmistress Ahhhhh...rriba!
I got that dancing rhythm
I got to move my feet
See how I'm dancing with them
Up and down de street.

All She got that dancing rhythm
She got to move her feet
See how she's dancing with them
Up and down de street.

Headmistress Let me tell you now ...

I got that rhythm, you know
The world around me start to spin
Listen to my heart as it go
Boom badda boom, oh such a din.

She got that rhythm, you know,
The world around her start to spin
Listen to her heart as it go
Boom badda boom, oh such a din.

Instrumental dance break

The Headmistress removes her long skirt to reveal a brightly coloured shorter one beneath. She takes off her shoes and throws them away. Two members of the cast hold up swords and she dances a limbo underneath

Hear the rhythm, feel the beat
Try to move your feet.
Hear the rhythm, feel the beat
Try to move your feet.
Hear the rhythm, feel the beat
Try to move your feet.
Hear the rhythm, feel the beat
Try to move your feet!

Headmistress Altogether now!
All We got that dancing rhythm
We got to move our feet
See how we're dancing with them
Up and down de street.

We got that rhythm, you know
The world around us start to spin
Listen to our hearts as they go...

Boom badda boom badda boom boom boom
Badda boom badda boom boom boom.
Badda boom, badda boom, badda boom boom boom
Badda boom Badda boom boom boom.
Badda boom, badda boom, badda boom boom boom
Badda boom badda boom boom boom.

Badda badda badda badda.
Badda badda badda badda
Badda badda Badda badda Badda badda Badda badda
Boooooooooooooom!

Instrumental dance break

The Headmistress blows her whistle in time to the music, and leads everyone in a conga line around the stage. The children sing along to the melody at one point during this instrumental break

>We got that rhythm, you know
>The world around us start to spin
>Listen to our hearts as they go ...
>
>Boom badda boom badda boom boom boom
>Badda boom badda boom boom boom

The cast divide into two singing groups

Group 1   **Group 2**
>Hear the rhythm, feel the beat   Badda boom badda boom
>Try to move your feet.   badda boom boom boom
>Hear the rhythm, feel the beat   Badda boom badda boom
>Try to move your feet.   Boom boom
>Hear the rhythm, feel the beat   Badda boom badda boom
>Try to move your feet.   Badda boom boom boom
>Hear the rhythm, feel the beat   Badda boom badda boom
>Try to move your feet.   Boom boom

All
>What a din!
>What a din!
>We got that crazy rhythm!
>
>Boom badda boom badda boom boom boom
>Badda boom badda boom boom boom
>Badda boom badda boom badda boom boom boom
>Badda boom! Boom! Boom!

No. 9a Curtain Calls

No. 9b Encore — Calypso Carnival Reprise

All
>We got that dancing rhythm
>We got to move our feet,
>See how we're dancing with them
>Up and down de street.

We got that rhythm, you know
The world around us start to spin,
Listen to our hearts as they go...

Boom badda boom badda boom boom boom
Badda boom badda boom boom boom.
Badda boom, badda boom, badda boom boom boom
Badda boom badda boom boom boom.
Badda boom, badda boom, badda boom boom boom
Badda boom badda boom boom boom.

Badda badda badda badda, Badda badda badda badda
Badda badda Badda badda, Badda badda Badda badda
Boooooooooooooom!

Instrumental dance break

What a din!
What a din!
We got that crazy rhythm!

Badda boom badda boom badda boom boom boom
Badda boom badda boom boom boom
Badda boom badda boom badda boom boom boom
Badda boom! Boom! Boom!

No. 9c Exit Music

FURNITURE & PROPERTY LIST

The following properties can be as simple or as elaborate as resources allow.

On stage: Palm trees
Tropical flowers
Market stalls. **On one:** flag with a bright yellow sun on a bright orange background
Crates and barrels
Rope
Small hut. *Inside it*: headmistress gown and mortar board, whistle on string, horn-rimmed spectacles; Carmen Miranda fruit head-dress. *Outside it*: stool; large book; wooden broom

Off stage: Crates of fruit and vegetables, fish, hats, and strings of bright flowers (**Islanders**)
Percussion instruments (**Islanders**)
Pirate Ship (*if required*)
Large, old trunk. Containing kitchen implements including wooden spoons, egg whisks, etc; two eyepatches; sink plunger; stuffed parrot; beach ball (inflated) (**Cuffee and Quashie**)
Swords (**Islanders**)
Skull and crossbones flag

Personal: **Pirates**: swords
Cuffee: banana
Pirate: knee bandage
Pirate: eyepatch

COSTUME PLOT

Islanders
Bright orange or red T-shirts with bright yellow smiling sun logo
Blue jeans or denim shorts
Bare feet

Pirates
Black T-shirts with white skull and crossbones logo
Black school trousers, torn off below the knee
Brown leather sword belt
Accessories: Pirates hats, eyepatches, bandages, etc

Captain George
Black T-shirt with white Skull & Crossbones logo
Black school trousers, torn off below the knee
Brown leather sword belt
Pirate hat with white skull and crossbones logo
Hoop earring

Fafa
Multi-coloured Hawaiian T-shirt
Bright green shorts
Bright red cap with bright yellow smiling sun logo

Ol' Manbo
Bright red shirt with bright yellow and blue patches
Long bright orange full skirt with white apron
Dark green scarf tied loosely around neck
Bright red, blue and yellow scarf tied around hair
Plain, black, flat pumps
Underdressed: Short, bright orange, wrap-over skirt
White cropped T-shirt

LIGHTING PLOT

Practical fittings required: footlights

To open: Dawn

Cue 1	**Fafa** enters *Dip main lights and add special on Fafa*	(Page 3)
Cue 2	**Fafa**: " I hate that." *Dip special and brighten main lighting*	(Page 4)
Cue 3	**Ol' Manbo** sits back down with her book *Dip main lighting and brighten special on* **Fafa**	(Page 4)
Cue 4	**Fafa:** " .... Cuffee and Quashie are arguing again…" *Dip special and brighten main lighting*	(Page 5)
Cue 5	**Quashie:** " ... we helped and everything …" *Dip main lighting and brighten special on* **Fafa**	(Page 5)
Cue 6	**Sun God**: (*voice over*) " ... all of its own …" *Bring up general, bright, full stage wash*	(Page 6)
Cue 7	At the end of song *Flash of lightning*	(Page 8)
Cue 8	**Ol' Manbo** moves away from the **Pirates** *General, morning, full stage wash*	(Page 8)
Cue 9	**First Mate**: "… left right, left right!" *General, bright, full stage wash*	(Page 10)
Cue 10	At the end of song *General, mid-morning, full stage wash*	(Page 12)
Cue 11	**Laura**: "... remember the words ..." *Dip main lights and add special on* **Fafa**	(Page 14)
Cue 12	**Fafa** exits *Cut special and brighten main lighting*	(Page 15)

Cue 13	At the end of song *Flash of lightning*	(Page 16)
Cue 14	**Fafa** appears within clearing smoke *General, bright, mid-morning full stage wash*	(Page 16)
Cue 15	**Fafa**: " ... you into a ..." *Flash of lightning*	(Page 17)
Cue 16	**Capt. George**: " ... the tales begin!" *General, bright full stage wash*	(Page 18)
Cue 17	**Capt. George**: " ... see you at sunset!" *General, afternoon, full stage wash*	(Page 21)
Cue 18	**Fafa**: " ... to turn these into ..." *Flash of lightning*	(Page 21)
Cue 19	**Fafa**: "Now to prepare — the spies!" *General stage wash dims; two open-white searchlights sweep the stage*	(Page 24)
Cue 20	**Cuffee** and **Quashie** mingle with the **Pirates** *Evening lighting, with storm brewing over the island. Lightning flashes in the distance*	(Page 26)
Cue 21	**Capt. George:** "... out there?". The **Pirates** look worried *Lightning; dark blue, shadowy, full stage cover*	(Page 27)
Cue 22	**Pirates**: *(singing)*"... they are?" They all laugh *Flash of lightning*	(Page 28)
Cue 23	**Pirates**: *(singing)*"... they are?" *Flash of lightning*	(Page 29)
Cue 24	Final big chord of song *Flash of lightning, much lighter than the first two bursts*	(Page 29)
Cue 25	Everyone screams *The Lights change to general, night time, full stage wash*	(Page 29)
Cue 26	**Fafa**: "… you into a ..." *Flash of lightning*	(Page 31)
Cue 27	**Fafa**: "… but, Dad ...!" *Flash of lightning*	(Page 31)

Lighting Plot

Cue 28	**Fafa**: "… hand me that flag!" *Flash of lightning. White lighting from footlights*	(Page 31)
Cue 29	**Fafa**: " … cannot defeat me!" *Flash of lightning*	(Page 34)
Cue 30	Music underscore No. 8a Dialogue ends *Flash of lightning*	(Page 34)
Cue 31	**Pirates**: "Headmistress!" *Bring up general, bright, full stage wash*	(Page 35)
Cue 32	**Sun God**: (*voice over*)" What did she say?!" *Flash of lightning*	(Page 38)
Cue 33	**Headmistress**: "Someone help me …!" *Flash of lightning*	(Page 38)
Cue 34	Song **No. 9 Calypso Carnival** begins *Colourful carnival lighting*	(Page 39)

EFFECTS PLOT

* See director's notes refering to Sun God's voice on page v

Cue 1	To open *Sound of breeze blowing softly through the trees and waves lapping gently at the beach*	(Page 1)
Cue 2	**Fafa**: "Happy day of the sun, dad." ***Sun God**'s voice dialogue pp 3-4*	(Page 3)
Cue 3	Special on **Fafa** brightens ***Sun God**'s voice dialogue pp 4-5*	(Page 4)
Cue 4	Special on **Fafa** brightens ***Sun God**'s voice dialogue p6*	(Page 6)
Cue 5	**Islanders** (*singing*): " ... each new ...". Lightning flash *Roll of thunder and if required cannon fire*	(Page 8)
Cue 6	Special on **Fafa** brightens ***Sun God**'s voice dialogue pp14-15*	(Page 14)
Cue 7	**Islanders** (*singing*): " Fafa!". Lightning flash *Roll of thunder and if required a cloud of smoke*	(Page 16)
Cue 8	**Fafa**:" ... turn you into a ...". Lightning flash *Roll of thunder*	(Page 17)
Cue 9	**Fafa**:" ... magic to turn these into ...". Lightning flash *Roll of thunder*	(Page 21)
Cue 10	**Cuffee** and **Quashie** slip out of hiding. Lightning flashes *Rolls of thunder*	(Page 26)
Cue 11	**Capt. George**: "... out there?". Lightning flash *Roll of thunder*	(Page 27)
Cue 12	**Pirates**: (*singing*) " ... they are?". Lightning flash *Roll of thunder*	(Page 28)

Effects Plot

Cue 13	**Pirates**: (*singing*) " ... they are?". Lightning flash *Roll of thunder*	(Page 29)
Cue 14	Final chord of song. Lightning flash *Roll of thunder much louder than before*	(Page 29)
Cue 15	**Fafa**: "… you into a ..." Lightning flash *Roll of thunder*	(Page 31)
Cue 16	**Fafa**: "… but, Dad ...!" Lightning flash *Roll of thunder*	(Page 31)
Cue 17	**Fafa**: "… hand me that flag!" Lightning flash *Roll of thunder*	(Page 31)
Cue 18	**Fafa**: " ... cannot defeat me!" Lightning flash *Roll of thunder*	(Page 34)
Cue 19	Music underscore ends. Lightning flash *Roll of thunder*	(Page 34)
Cue 20	**Fafa** chant ends with a loud "Boo!" *Thunder rumbles*	(Page 35)
Cue 21	The hut begins to shakes. *Smoke pours out of the door (optional)*	(Page 35)
Cue 22	**Fafa**: " Dad?" ***Sun God**'s *voice dialogue p.38*	(Page 38)
Cue 23	**Sun God**: (*voice over*)"What did she say?!" Lightning flash *Roll of thunder*	(Page 38)
Cue 24	**Headmistress**:"Someone help me ...!" Lightning flash *Roll of thunder*	(Page 38)

MADE AND PRINTED IN GREAT BRITAIN BY
LATIMER TREND & COMPANY LTD PLYMOUTH
MADE IN ENGLAND